EMMANUEL JOSEPH

Eclipsed Emotions, The Interplay of Astronomy, Literature, and Psychological Depth

Copyright © 2025 by Emmanuel Joseph

All rights reserved. No part of this publication may be reproduced, stored or transmitted in any form or by any means, electronic, mechanical, photocopying, recording, scanning, or otherwise without written permission from the publisher. It is illegal to copy this book, post it to a website, or distribute it by any other means without permission.

First edition

*This book was professionally typeset on Reedsy.
Find out more at reedsy.com*

Contents

1	Chapter 1: Celestial Beginnings	1
2	Chapter 2: Cosmic Influences on Human Emotion	3
3	Chapter 3: Literary Reflections of Astronomical Themes	5
4	Chapter 4: The Moon as a Literary Symbol	7
5	Chapter 5: Solar Symbolism in Literature	9
6	Chapter 6: Stars as Metaphors for Hope and Guidance	11
7	Chapter 7: Celestial Omens and Human Fate	13
8	Chapter 8: The Interstellar Journey as a Metaphor for...	15
9	Chapter 9: The Eclipse as a Symbol of Transformation	17
10	Chapter 10: The Milky Way as a Symbol of Connection	19
11	Chapter 11: Celestial Cycles and Human Resilience	21
12	Chapter 12: The Cosmos and the Human Psyche	23
13	Chapter 13: The Influence of Comets in Literature	25
14	Chapter 14: The Role of the Night Sky in Folklore and Myth	27
15	Chapter 15: The Future of Celestial Exploration and Its...	29

1

Chapter 1: Celestial Beginnings

The allure of the night sky has long captivated human imagination. From the earliest civilizations, people have looked to the stars for guidance, inspiration, and a sense of wonder. The cosmos, with its vastness and mystery, has served as a backdrop for countless stories and mythologies. Ancient cultures, such as the Babylonians and Egyptians, meticulously recorded the movements of celestial bodies, seeking to understand the universe and their place within it. This fascination with the heavens is deeply rooted in our collective consciousness, providing a rich tapestry upon which to weave tales of emotion and introspection.

Astronomy, the scientific study of celestial objects, has evolved over millennia, shedding light on the intricate dance of planets, stars, and galaxies. The advent of telescopes and advanced observational techniques has allowed us to peer deeper into the cosmos than ever before. As our understanding of the universe expands, so too does our appreciation for its complexity and beauty. This ever-growing knowledge serves as a foundation for exploring the connections between the cosmos and the human psyche.

The interplay between astronomy and literature is a testament to the power of storytelling. Writers have long drawn upon celestial imagery to convey profound emotions and ideas. The night sky, with its constellations and celestial events, provides a rich source of metaphors and symbols. From the romantic musings of poets to the speculative worlds of science fiction, literature has harnessed the power of the cosmos to evoke a sense of awe, wonder, and introspection.

   Psychological depth is another crucial aspect of this interplay. The vastness of the universe often mirrors the complexities of the human mind. Our emotions, thoughts, and experiences can feel as boundless and mysterious as the cosmos itself. By examining the connections between astronomy, literature, and psychology, we can gain a deeper understanding of our own inner worlds. This exploration invites us to reflect on the nature of existence, the meaning of our emotions, and our place within the grand tapestry of the universe.

2

Chapter 2: Cosmic Influences on Human Emotion

The influence of celestial phenomena on human emotions is a fascinating area of study. Throughout history, people have attributed significant events and emotions to the movements of celestial bodies. The changing phases of the moon, the alignment of planets, and the appearance of comets have all been seen as harbingers of change and transformation. This belief in the connection between the cosmos and human emotions is deeply ingrained in various cultures and continues to shape our understanding of the world.

Astrology, the study of the influence of celestial bodies on human affairs, is a prime example of this connection. While often dismissed as pseudoscience, astrology has played a significant role in shaping human history and culture. The zodiac, with its twelve signs, offers a framework for understanding personality traits and predicting future events. The alignment of planets at the time of one's birth is believed to influence an individual's character and life path. This belief in cosmic influence can provide comfort and guidance, helping people navigate the complexities of their emotions and experiences.

Literature has long explored the interplay between celestial phenomena and human emotion. The works of writers such as William Shakespeare, Edgar Allan Poe, and Virginia Woolf are replete with celestial imagery. The moon, stars, and planets serve as powerful symbols, evoking a range of emotions and ideas. Shakespeare's "Romeo and Juliet," for example, uses the imagery of the night sky to convey the intensity of the lovers' emotions. The moon, a symbol of change and transformation, reflects the tumultuous nature of their love and the inevitability of their tragic fate.

The psychological implications of this cosmic connection are profound. The vastness of the universe can evoke a sense of awe and wonder, inspiring introspection and self-discovery. At the same time, the enormity of the cosmos can also elicit feelings of insignificance and existential dread. By examining the ways in which celestial phenomena influence human emotions, we can gain insight into the complexities of our own inner worlds. This exploration invites us to reflect on the nature of our emotions, the meaning of our experiences, and our place within the grand tapestry of the universe.

3

Chapter 3: Literary Reflections of Astronomical Themes

Literature has long served as a mirror, reflecting the intricacies of the human experience. Astronomical themes, with their inherent sense of wonder and mystery, provide a rich source of inspiration for writers. From ancient epics to contemporary novels, the cosmos has played a central role in shaping literary landscapes. These celestial motifs not only enhance storytelling but also offer profound insights into the human condition.

One of the earliest examples of astronomical themes in literature can be found in the epic of Gilgamesh. This ancient Mesopotamian text, often considered the world's first great work of literature, features celestial imagery that underscores the protagonist's quest for immortality. The stars and constellations serve as symbols of the divine and the eternal, highlighting the transience of human life and the enduring nature of the cosmos. This interplay between the heavens and the earthly realm underscores the timeless nature of human aspirations and struggles.

In more recent literary works, astronomical themes continue to captivate readers. Science fiction, in particular, has embraced the cosmos as a canvas for exploring complex ideas and emotions. Authors such as Isaac Asimov, Arthur C. Clarke, and Ursula K. Le Guin have used the vastness of space to delve into questions of identity, morality, and the nature of existence. The imaginative worlds they create offer a unique perspective on the human experience, inviting readers to ponder the mysteries of the universe and their place within it.

The psychological depth of these literary explorations cannot be overstated. The cosmos, with its infinite possibilities, serves as a metaphor for the boundless nature of the human mind. The vastness of space mirrors the complexities of our emotions, thoughts, and experiences. By engaging with astronomical themes in literature, we are invited to reflect on our own inner worlds and the broader questions of existence. This interplay between the cosmos and the human psyche offers a profound lens through which to explore the depths of our emotions and the meaning of our lives.

4

Chapter 4: The Moon as a Literary Symbol

The moon, with its ever-changing phases and ethereal glow, has long been a source of inspiration for writers and poets. As a literary symbol, the moon embodies a range of emotions and ideas, from romance and mystery to melancholy and transformation. This celestial body, with its enigmatic presence, serves as a powerful motif in literature, offering a window into the depths of the human psyche.

In romantic literature, the moon often symbolizes love and longing. Poets such as Percy Bysshe Shelley and John Keats used lunar imagery to convey the intensity of their emotions. The moon's silvery light, casting a soft glow on the landscape, evokes a sense of intimacy and tenderness. In Shelley's "To the Moon," the poet addresses the celestial body as a confidant, sharing his feelings of yearning and melancholy. The moon becomes a silent witness to the poet's emotions, reflecting the ephemeral nature of love and the passage of time.

The moon also plays a central role in Gothic literature, where it symbolizes mystery and the supernatural. In works such as Mary Shelley's "Frankenstein" and Bram Stoker's "Dracula," the moonlit night serves as a backdrop for scenes of horror and intrigue. The moon's pale light casts an eerie glow, heightening the sense of unease and foreboding. This use of lunar imagery underscores the themes of darkness and the unknown, inviting readers to explore the shadowy realms of the human mind.

Psychologically, the moon's cyclical nature mirrors the rhythms of human emotions. Just as the moon waxes and wanes, our feelings ebb and flow, reflecting the ever-changing landscape of our inner worlds. The moon's phases serve as a metaphor for transformation and renewal, reminding us of the impermanence of our emotions and experiences. By engaging with lunar imagery in literature, we are invited to reflect on the cyclical nature of our own lives and the deeper meanings that lie beneath the surface.

5

Chapter 5: Solar Symbolism in Literature

The sun, with its life-giving energy and radiant light, has long been a powerful symbol in literature. As the center of our solar system, the sun represents warmth, vitality, and illumination. Its presence in literary works often serves to underscore themes of growth, enlightenment, and the passage of time. By examining solar symbolism, we can gain a deeper understanding of the interplay between the cosmos and the human experience.

In classical literature, the sun is frequently associated with the divine. In Homer's "The Iliad," the sun god Helios drives his chariot across the sky, symbolizing the eternal cycle of day and night. This celestial imagery highlights the connection between the heavens and the earthly realm, underscoring the influence of the divine on human affairs. The sun's radiant light serves as a metaphor for truth and enlightenment, guiding characters on their journeys and illuminating the path to self-discovery.

In more contemporary works, the sun continues to play a central role in shaping literary narratives. Authors such as Ernest Hemingway and F. Scott Fitzgerald use solar imagery to convey themes of hope, ambition, and the passage of time. In Hemingway's "The Sun Also Rises," the sun's relentless journey across the sky serves as a backdrop for the protagonist's quest for meaning and purpose. The sun's cyclical nature mirrors the characters' struggles and triumphs, reminding readers of the enduring nature of the human spirit.

The psychological implications of solar symbolism are profound. The sun's light, with its warmth and vitality, represents the life force within each of us. Its presence in literature serves as a reminder of our own potential for growth and transformation. By engaging with solar imagery, we are invited to reflect on the sources of light and energy in our own lives, and the ways in which we can harness this power to illuminate our paths and achieve our goals.

6

Chapter 6: Stars as Metaphors for Hope and Guidance

Stars, with their constant presence in the night sky, have long served as symbols of hope and guidance in literature. These celestial bodies, shining brightly from unimaginable distances, evoke a sense of wonder and inspiration. Throughout history, stars have been used to navigate both literal and metaphorical journeys, guiding characters and readers alike through the complexities of life and emotion.

In ancient mythology, stars were often associated with the divine and the supernatural. The constellations, with their intricate patterns and stories, provided a celestial map for understanding the world. The Greek myth of Orion, for example, tells the story of a great hunter who was placed among the stars after his death. This transformation into a constellation symbolizes the eternal nature of heroism and the enduring power of memory. The stars, as markers of the divine, offer a sense of hope and guidance, reminding us of the larger forces at play in the universe.

In more modern literature, stars continue to serve as powerful symbols of hope and inspiration. In F. Scott Fitzgerald's "The Great Gatsby," the green light at the end of Daisy's dock is often interpreted as a metaphor for Gatsby's aspirations and dreams. The light, shining across the water, represents the unattainable ideal that drives Gatsby's actions and ultimately leads to his downfall. This use of stellar imagery underscores the themes of ambition, desire, and the human capacity for hope.

Psychologically, stars represent the guiding principles that illuminate our paths and inspire us to reach for greater heights. Their constancy and brilliance serve as reminders of the potential within each of us. By engaging with stellar imagery in literature, we are invited to reflect on our own sources of hope and inspiration. This exploration of the cosmos and the human psyche offers a profound lens through which to examine the interplay between our inner worlds and the larger universe.

7

Chapter 7: Celestial Omens and Human Fate

The belief in celestial omens and their influence on human fate is a theme that runs deep in literature and culture. Throughout history, people have looked to the heavens for signs and portents, seeking to understand the future and make sense of the present. Celestial events such as eclipses, comets, and meteor showers have been interpreted as harbingers of change, signaling both good fortune and impending doom.

In ancient civilizations, celestial omens played a crucial role in shaping decisions and actions. The Babylonians, for example, meticulously recorded the movements of celestial bodies, believing that these patterns could predict future events. The appearance of a comet or an eclipse was often seen as a divine message, guiding rulers and individuals alike. This belief in the connection between the heavens and human fate is reflected in various literary works, where celestial omens serve as powerful symbols of destiny and transformation.

Shakespeare's "Julius Caesar" is a prime example of the use of celestial omens in literature. The play is replete with references to strange and ominous events in the sky, foreshadowing the assassination of Caesar and the chaos that ensues. The appearance of a comet, the unusual brightness of the stars, and the lunar eclipse all serve as metaphors for the upheaval and turmoil that will soon unfold. These celestial signs heighten the sense of foreboding and underscore the themes of fate and destiny.

The psychological implications of celestial omens are profound. The belief in cosmic signs speaks to our innate desire for meaning and understanding in an uncertain world. By examining the ways in which celestial events are interpreted as omens, we can gain insight into the human psyche and our need for guidance and reassurance. This exploration of the cosmos and human fate invites us to reflect on the larger forces that shape our lives and the ways in which we navigate the uncertainties of existence.

8

Chapter 8: The Interstellar Journey as a Metaphor for Self-Discovery

The concept of the interstellar journey, with its boundless possibilities and unknown destinations, has long served as a powerful metaphor for self-discovery in literature. The vastness of space, with its infinite horizons and uncharted territories, mirrors the complexities of the human mind and the journey of personal growth. By embarking on a voyage through the cosmos, characters and readers alike are invited to explore the depths of their own inner worlds.

Science fiction, in particular, has embraced the theme of the interstellar journey as a means of exploring identity and self-discovery. In Arthur C. Clarke's "2001: A Space Odyssey," the protagonist, Dave Bowman, embarks on a journey through space that ultimately leads to a profound transformation. As he navigates the unknown reaches of the cosmos, Bowman confronts his own limitations and transcends his human form, symbolizing the potential for growth and evolution within each of us. This interstellar journey serves as a metaphor for the quest for self-understanding and the search for meaning in an ever-changing universe.

In more contemporary works, the theme of the interstellar journey continues to captivate readers. In Octavia Butler's "Parable of the Sower," the protagonist, Lauren Olamina, undertakes a journey through a dystopian landscape, seeking a new home and a sense of purpose. This journey, both physical and emotional, mirrors Lauren's inner quest for self-discovery and empowerment. The challenges and discoveries she encounters along the way serve as catalysts for personal growth and transformation.

The psychological depth of the interstellar journey lies in its ability to evoke a sense of wonder and introspection. The vastness of space, with its infinite possibilities, invites us to reflect on our own potential for growth and self-discovery. By engaging with the theme of the interstellar journey, we are encouraged to explore the depths of our own inner worlds and to embrace the unknown with curiosity and courage. This exploration of the cosmos and the human psyche offers a profound lens through which to examine the interplay between our inner journeys and the larger universe.

9

Chapter 9: The Eclipse as a Symbol of Transformation

The phenomenon of an eclipse, with its dramatic interplay of light and shadow, has long been a source of fascination and inspiration in literature. As a celestial event, the eclipse symbolizes moments of profound change and transformation, both in the natural world and within the human psyche. The temporary obscuring of the sun or moon serves as a powerful metaphor for the cycles of growth, renewal, and self-discovery that shape our lives.

In ancient mythology, eclipses were often seen as omens of significant events. The Greeks, for example, believed that an eclipse signaled the wrath of the gods, while the Chinese viewed it as a cosmic battle between celestial beings. These interpretations highlight the sense of awe and wonder that eclipses evoke, reminding us of the larger forces at play in the universe. This celestial phenomenon, with its fleeting nature, serves as a reminder of the impermanence of our experiences and the constant potential for transformation.

In literature, the eclipse is frequently used as a symbol of personal and emotional transformation. In Gabriel Garcia Marquez's "One Hundred Years of Solitude," the eclipse serves as a turning point in the narrative, marking moments of revelation and change for the characters. The interplay of light and shadow mirrors the complexities of their inner worlds, reflecting the themes of memory, identity, and the passage of time. This use of eclipse imagery underscores the cyclical nature of existence and the potential for renewal and growth.

Psychologically, the eclipse represents the process of introspection and self-discovery. The temporary obscuring of light invites us to explore the shadowy realms of our own minds, confronting our fears, doubts, and unresolved emotions. By engaging with the symbolism of the eclipse, we are encouraged to embrace moments of darkness as opportunities for growth and transformation. This exploration of the cosmos and the human psyche offers a profound lens through which to examine the interplay between our inner worlds and the larger universe.

10

Chapter 10: The Milky Way as a Symbol of Connection

The Milky Way, with its sprawling expanse of stars and cosmic dust, has long served as a symbol of connection and unity in literature. This celestial phenomenon, visible as a luminous band across the night sky, evokes a sense of wonder and belonging. The Milky Way's vastness and complexity remind us of the interconnectedness of all things, both in the cosmos and within our own lives.

In ancient cultures, the Milky Way was often seen as a bridge between the earthly and divine realms. The Greeks referred to it as the "Galactic River," while the Chinese viewed it as the "Silver River" that connected the heavens. These interpretations highlight the sense of connection and continuity that the Milky Way represents, reminding us of the larger forces that bind us together. This celestial phenomenon serves as a powerful metaphor for the interconnectedness of all things, both in the natural world and within the human experience.

In literature, the Milky Way often symbolizes the ties that bind characters to one another and to the larger universe. In John Steinbeck's "The Grapes of Wrath," the Milky Way serves as a backdrop for the Joad family's journey, symbolizing their hopes and dreams for a better future. The luminous band of stars represents the interconnectedness of their experiences, highlighting the themes of family, resilience, and the search for meaning. This use of celestial imagery underscores the sense of unity and connection that defines the human experience.

Psychologically, the Milky Way represents the web of connections that shape our lives. The vastness of this cosmic phenomenon mirrors the complexities of our relationships, thoughts, and emotions. By engaging with the symbolism of the Milky Way, we are invited to reflect on the ways in which we are connected to others and the larger universe. This exploration of the cosmos and the human psyche offers a profound lens through which to examine the interplay between our inner worlds and the broader tapestry of existence.

11

Chapter 11: Celestial Cycles and Human Resilience

The cyclical nature of celestial events, such as the phases of the moon and the changing seasons, has long served as a metaphor for human resilience in literature. These cycles, with their inherent rhythm and predictability, mirror the ebb and flow of human experiences. The constancy of these celestial patterns offers a sense of stability and continuity, reminding us of our own capacity to endure and adapt.

In classical literature, the changing seasons often symbolize the stages of human life. In Shakespeare's "The Winter's Tale," the cycle of the seasons reflects the themes of loss, redemption, and renewal. The harshness of winter gives way to the promise of spring, symbolizing the characters' journey from sorrow to hope. This use of seasonal imagery underscores the resilience of the human spirit, highlighting our ability to overcome adversity and embrace new beginnings.

In more contemporary works, the cyclical nature of celestial events continues to inspire themes of resilience and transformation. In Toni Morrison's "Beloved," the changing seasons serve as a backdrop for the protagonist's journey of healing and self-discovery. The cycle of growth and decay mirrors the characters' emotional struggles and triumphs, offering a powerful metaphor for the process of personal growth and renewal. This use of celestial imagery underscores the themes of resilience and the enduring nature of the human spirit.

Psychologically, the cyclical nature of celestial events reminds us of our own capacity for resilience and renewal. Just as the moon waxes and wanes and the seasons change, our emotions and experiences follow their own patterns of growth and transformation. By engaging with the symbolism of celestial cycles, we are invited to reflect on the ways in which we navigate the challenges and uncertainties of life. This exploration of the cosmos and the human psyche offers a profound lens through which to examine the interplay between our inner worlds and the broader rhythms of existence.

12

Chapter 12: The Cosmos and the Human Psyche

The relationship between the cosmos and the human psyche is a theme that transcends time and culture. The vastness of the universe, with its infinite possibilities and mysteries, serves as a powerful metaphor for the complexities of the human mind. By exploring the connections between the cosmos and our inner worlds, we can gain a deeper understanding of our own emotions, thoughts, and experiences.

In ancient mythology, the cosmos was often seen as a reflection of the human psyche. The Greek myth of Pandora's box, for example, uses celestial imagery to explore themes of curiosity, hope, and despair. The stars, scattered across the night sky, symbolize the remnants of hope that remain after Pandora's box is opened. This interplay between the heavens and the human mind highlights the ways in which our inner worlds are shaped by the larger forces of the universe.

In modern literature, the cosmos continues to serve as a powerful metaphor for the human psyche. In Carl Sagan's "Contact," the protagonist's journey to the stars mirrors her quest for understanding and self-discovery. The vastness of space, with its infinite possibilities, represents the boundless nature of the human mind. This exploration of the cosmos invites readers to reflect on their own inner worlds and the mysteries that lie within.

The psychological implications of this cosmic connection are profound. The universe, with its vastness and complexity, serves as a mirror for the depths of our own minds. By engaging with celestial imagery and themes, we are invited to explore the intricacies of our emotions, thoughts, and experiences. This exploration of the cosmos and the human psyche offers a profound lens through which to examine the interplay between our inner worlds and the larger universe.

13

Chapter 13: The Influence of Comets in Literature

Comets, with their bright tails and sudden appearances, have long fascinated humanity. These celestial wanderers have been considered omens, harbingers of change, and symbols of unpredictability. In literature, comets often represent transformative events and the potential for disruption and renewal. Their fleeting presence in the night sky serves as a powerful metaphor for the transient nature of life and the unexpected moments that shape our destinies.

Historically, comets have been viewed with both awe and apprehension. Ancient civilizations saw them as divine messengers, bringing news of significant events. The appearance of a comet was often interpreted as a sign of impending change, whether positive or negative. This belief in the transformative power of comets is reflected in various literary works, where they serve as catalysts for character development and plot progression.

In Mark Twain's "The Adventures of Huckleberry Finn," the appearance of a comet symbolizes a turning point in the protagonist's journey. The celestial event underscores the themes of change and transformation, highlighting the characters' growth and the shifting dynamics of their relationships. The comet's sudden and dramatic presence mirrors the unpredictable nature of their adventures, reminding readers of the ever-changing landscape of human experience.

Psychologically, comets represent the unexpected moments that disrupt our lives and force us to adapt. Their fleeting nature serves as a reminder of the impermanence of our experiences and the potential for growth and transformation. By engaging with the symbolism of comets, we are encouraged to embrace change and view it as an opportunity for self-discovery and renewal. This exploration of the cosmos and the human psyche offers a profound lens through which to examine the interplay between our inner worlds and the larger universe.

14

Chapter 14: The Role of the Night Sky in Folklore and Myth

The night sky, with its myriad stars and celestial phenomena, has played a central role in folklore and myth across cultures. These stories, passed down through generations, reflect humanity's fascination with the cosmos and our desire to make sense of the universe. The night sky serves as a canvas upon which tales of gods, heroes, and mythical creatures are painted, offering insights into the values, beliefs, and emotions of different cultures.

In many indigenous cultures, the night sky is seen as a realm of spirits and ancestors. The stars are believed to be the souls of the departed, watching over the living and guiding them through life. These celestial beings play an integral role in the oral traditions and mythologies of these communities, providing a sense of connection to the past and continuity for the future. The night sky becomes a bridge between the earthly and the divine, reminding us of the interconnectedness of all things.

In classical mythology, the night sky is populated with gods and heroes who have been immortalized as constellations. The story of Perseus and Andromeda, for example, is etched into the night sky as a reminder of bravery and sacrifice. These constellations serve as celestial maps, guiding sailors and travelers on their journeys. The tales associated with these stars offer valuable lessons and moral guidance, reflecting the cultural values of the societies that created them.

Psychologically, the night sky in folklore and myth represents the mysteries of the human mind and the unknown aspects of our inner worlds. The stars and celestial phenomena symbolize the dreams, fears, and aspirations that shape our experiences. By engaging with these stories, we are invited to explore the depths of our own psyches and the universal themes that connect us all. This exploration of the cosmos and the human psyche offers a profound lens through which to examine the interplay between our inner worlds and the larger universe.

15

Chapter 15: The Future of Celestial Exploration and Its Impact on Human Consciousness

As we stand on the brink of a new era of celestial exploration, the impact of these endeavors on human consciousness cannot be understated. The advancements in space travel and technology have opened up new possibilities for understanding the universe and our place within it. These explorations have the potential to reshape our perspectives, challenging us to rethink our assumptions about life, existence, and the cosmos.

The recent achievements in space exploration, such as the Mars rover missions and the discovery of exoplanets, have sparked a renewed interest in the cosmos. These milestones not only expand our scientific knowledge but also inspire a sense of wonder and curiosity. The possibility of finding life beyond Earth or colonizing other planets invites us to imagine new futures and reconsider the boundaries of human potential.

In literature, the theme of celestial exploration offers a rich source of inspiration for envisioning the future. Science fiction authors such as Kim Stanley Robinson and Liu Cixin have explored the implications of space travel on human society and consciousness. Their works invite readers to contemplate the ethical, philosophical, and psychological challenges that come with venturing into the unknown. The imaginative worlds they create serve as mirrors for our own hopes, fears, and aspirations.

Psychologically, the prospect of celestial exploration invites us to expand our horizons and embrace new possibilities. The vastness of space, with its infinite potential, mirrors the boundless nature of the human mind. By engaging with the themes of space travel and exploration, we are encouraged to think beyond our immediate experiences and consider the larger questions of existence. This exploration of the cosmos and the human psyche offers a profound lens through which to examine the interplay between our inner worlds and the future of humanity.

Book Description

"Eclipsed Emotions: The Interplay of Astronomy, Literature, and Psychological Depth" is a captivating exploration of the profound connections between the cosmos and the human experience. Through twelve thought-provoking chapters, this book delves into the ways in which celestial phenomena have inspired literature, shaped cultural beliefs, and influenced our understanding of the human psyche.

From the ancient myths and folklore that populate the night sky to the modern tales of space exploration, "Eclipsed Emotions" weaves together a rich tapestry of stories and insights. Each chapter explores a different aspect of the interplay between astronomy and literature, revealing the ways in which celestial symbols and themes mirror the complexities of human emotions and experiences.

The book also examines the psychological implications of our fascination with the cosmos. The vastness of the universe, with its infinite possibilities and mysteries, serves as a powerful metaphor for the depths of the human mind. By exploring the connections between the celestial and the psychological, readers are invited to reflect on their own inner worlds and the broader rhythms of existence.

Whether you are a lover of literature, a stargazer, or simply curious about the mysteries of the universe, "Eclipsed Emotions" offers a compelling journey through the cosmos and the human psyche. This book invites you to look to

CHAPTER 15: THE FUTURE OF CELESTIAL EXPLORATION AND ITS...

the stars for inspiration and to discover the profound connections that bind us to the universe and each other.